THE 125 MOST ASKED QUESTIONS ABOUT ADOPTION

(AND THE ANSWERS)

THE 125 MOST ASKED QUESTIONS ABOUT ADOPTION

(AND THE ANSWERS)

Paul Baldwin

William Morrow and Company, Inc.

New York

It is the policy of William Morrow and Company, Inc., and its imprints and affiliates, recognizing the importance of preserving what has been written, to print the books we publish on acid-free paper, and we exert our best efforts to that end.

Library of Congress Cataloging-in-Publication Data

Baldwin, Paul.
    The 125 most asked questions about adoption / by Paul Baldwin.
        p.   cm.
    Includes bibliographical references and index.
    ISBN 0-688-11530-6
    1. Adoption—Miscellanea.   2. Adoption—United States—
Miscellanea.   I. Title.   II. Title: One hundred twenty-five most
asked questions about adoption.   III. Title: One hundred and
twenty-five most asked questions about adoption.
HV875.B318   1993
362.7'34'0973—dc20   92-42607
                                                              CIP

Printed in the United States of America

First Edition

1   2   3   4   5   6   7   8   9   10

BOOK DESIGN BY SUSAN HOOD

Contents

The Birth of Modern Adoption

Q. I am aware that the concept of adoption is very ancient, some form of it existing as far back as the Greeks and Romans of ancient times. *When did modern adoption laws first come into existence in the United States?*

A. Adoption in some form or another is indeed a very ancient practice. But often it consisted of what amounted to an indentured servant role for the adopted child. The idea that adopted children were to be treated as though they were in fact biological offspring was first codified into law in this country in 1851. The first laws that called for written consent of the birth parents, or parent, and full legal separation of the adopted child from the birth parents by judicial decree were enacted in Massachusetts, always one of the most forward-looking states in terms of social regulation. It was no accident that it was also in Massachusetts that the first private adoption agency, called the Home of the Happy Wanderers, was formed during the Civil War to find homes for the many orphans of that conflict.

How Many Adoptions a Year?

Q. Although the population of the United States keeps growing, I have heard that the number of adoptions in this country has actually decreased. *What has been the trend in numbers of adoptions over the past several decades?*

A. In 1957, there were 91,000 adoptions, and the number increased each year thereafter, reaching a peak in 1970, when there were 175,000 adoptions. The number then began to decline quite steadily until the level now is about where it was in the late 1950s. These numbers are approximate, however—because the federal government doesn't keep track of adoptions, it requires a lot of scrambling around to come up with even ballpark numbers.

It is interesting to note that the number of adoptions began to drop three years before the Supreme Court's hotly debated *Roe* v. *Wade* decision. This drop is widely regarded to be the result of increasing use of birth control. But the decline since 1974 is clearly affected by the right to abortion.

How Many Total Adoptees?

Q. As an adopted child, now in my mid-twenties, I have encountered a lot of other adoptees over the years. It's curious how we
seem to find one another. *How many adoptees are there in the
United States?*

A. Many adoptees comment on the fact that they seem to know
quite a number of other people who were adopted. Partially, this
may be because if one person is very open about being adopted,
other people who might be less likely to say they are adopted
except to good friends will feel entirely comfortable about saying
"me too" even to someone they don't know well. But there is also
the fact that there are a lot of adopted people. The generally
accepted estimate is six million, although that figure is more an
extrapolation than a real statistic.

Choosing Traditional or Open Adoption

Q. We know several people who were traditional adoptees, with no knowledge of their biological parents, who seem very well-adjusted and happy with their lives. But we have also heard a number of people tout open or experimental adoption as a more realistic and healthy alternative. *Are there any studies that indicate how traditional and open adoption compare in terms of the overall well-being of the adoptees themselves?*

A. Not yet. Traditional adoption has a long track record and is known to be successful in the great majority of cases. Open—or experimental—adoption, which involves communication between the birth mother and the adoptive parents, quite often including actual contact, is a more recent development, at least on any scale. Those who advocate open adoption have a firm belief that it is more honest and thus more likely to promote a child's emotional health, but there are many experts who feel that it can be a volatile situation, especially in cases where the birth mother (and possibly father) are given a great deal of access to the adopted child.

Since there is not yet enough information to make objective comparisons, the choice for prospective adoptive parents must be based on what they feel comfortable with as a couple.

Terminology Battles

Q. We are on the verge of trying to adopt a child, and try to pick up information on the subject at every turn. At a recent large gathering we were talking with a couple who have a three-year-old adopted son. This was a traditional adoption and when we used the term "open adoption," which is the option we are seriously considering, they practically bit our heads off and said it was properly called experimental rather than open. *Why is the term "open adoption" a touchy subject?*

A. Because many traditional adoption organizations (as well as adoptive parents who have gone the traditional route) feel that the term "open adoption" is essentially a slur against traditional adoption, suggesting that traditional adoption is "closed." And they are right: Open adoption advocates tend to regard traditional adoption as "secretive," "unhealthy," and a number of other unsavory things. The traditional adoption people, on the other hand, sometimes dismiss open adoption with words like "nutty." This battle over terminology might be compared to the one over the terms "pro-abortion" and "pro-choice." Both sides are trying to get the public relations upper hand with the use of different terms.

Continued Support for the Birth Mother

Q. I was shocked to learn that my nephew and his wife are sending a monthly check to the birth mother of the baby girl they adopted nearly a year ago. The adoption was supposedly legal in every way, so I can't understand this at all. It sounds like they *bought* the baby—and the mother! *Can it possibly be legal to pay the birth mother a stipend forever?*

A. Obviously, your nephew and his wife took the open adoption route to finding a child. It is legal in terms of open adoptions to pay a birth mother after she relinquishes a child. There are cases in which the adoptive parents may be helping the birth mother to pay for college, but there are also situations in which the birth mother has simply cut herself a very good deal. Birth mothers have been known to take advantage of couples desperate to adopt. It all depends on the particular contract between the birth mother and the adoptive parents as to how long the payments continue, but there is always a cutoff time. Such payments do not go on forever.

Open Adoption Visitation Rights

Q. Against my wishes, my unwed daughter put her baby girl up for adoption. This breaks my heart. *Since it was an open adoption, do I have any visitation rights as the biological grandmother?*

A. In almost all states, some provisions exist concerning visitation rights for biological grandparents in an open adoption situation, but the rules vary a good deal. Visitation rights by relatives in cases of open adoption have been a subject of much debate in recent years. Many argue that biological relatives would be an intrusion on the child's "new life" with the adopted family, causing needless confusion. This might be particularly true in your case, since you were so much against the adoption—what they consider as meddling is not something the adoptive parents have to put up with.

Independent Adoption

Q. My former college roommate is unmarried and pregnant. She is not "mother material" and she knows it, so she asked my husband and me if we would raise the child as our own. We are childless and would love to be "instant" parents. *Is it legal to simply turn a baby over to other people?*

A. Yes, this form of adoption—which is called either independent adoption or private adoption—is legal in most states. Independent adoptions, which sidestep the services of a licensed agency, are as common as adoptions from private agencies. Some experts frown on independent adoptions because they feel they involve an increased chance of the birth mother attempting to reclaim the child at a later date. Certainly, a lawyer should be used to make the adoption fully legal.

"Informal Adoption"

Q. My teenage daughter is pregnant and plans to put her baby up for adoption. She is taking this whole situation very casually, so I am trying to help out, mostly by reading anything I can get my hands on about the subject. I have read about open, traditional, and independent adoptions, but my daughter threw a new term at me the other day. *What on earth is "informal adoption"?*

A. This form of adoption is fairly common in rural areas. What it means is that the baby is given over, usually to a relative or friend, without going through an adoption agency. There is no legal process involved, as the word "informal" implies, and that can lead to trouble down the line.

Whose Interests Come First?

Q. In exploring various possible ways of going about adopting a child, we get the feeling that some modes of adoption put different parties in greater control of the situation, but we can't seem to quite pin it all down. *Is there a clear pattern that suggests whose interests usually come first in the various approaches to adoption available?*

A. Yes, there is. For a licensed agency, whether public or private, the interests of the child come first—the child is the agency's "client." A lawyer handling an independent adoption is able to get around many of the controls that are in force at agencies, and thus is able to put the interests of the adoptive couple first. In these cases, the adoptive couple become the main clients. Because of the very nature of open adoption, however, in which the birth mother has the chance to select the adoptive parents she likes best, she is given the opportunity to exercise the greatest degree of control.

Related and Unrelated
Adoptions

Q. I am now twenty years old. I was adopted by an aunt and uncle when I was seven, following the death of both my parents in an automobile accident. When I was growing up in Minnesota, most of the adopted kids I knew had also been adopted by relatives. I am now going to college in Oregon, and it seems to be the other way around: Most adopted people seem to have parents they are not related to by blood. *Do the number of related and unrelated adoptions vary a lot in different parts of the country?*

A. In the vast majority of states, the number of children adopted by relatives is greater than unrelated adoptions, including unrelated adoption by public agencies, private agencies, and adoption by private individuals. Your home state of Minnesota has one of the highest rates of adoption by relatives, 71.4 percent according to the latest available figures. There are only ten states where the number of unrelated adoptions is higher than related ones: New Jersey, Ohio, Illinois, Idaho, New Mexico, California, Delaware, Maryland, Nevada, and, yes, Oregon.

The generally high rate of adoption by relatives is of course one reason why couples seeking to adopt an unrelated child have to wait so long before an adoption goes through.

Free for Adoption

Q. My granddaughter is seventeen, unmarried, and pregnant. She wants to go to college and is giving the baby up for adoption through a private agency. She says that when she signs the papers with the agency (her boyfriend is signing too) the baby will be "free for adoption." *What exactly does "free for adoption" mean?*

A. It simply means that the birth mother (and the father, if he is party to the proceedings) is relinquishing her rights as parent of the child. Once the documents are signed with the agency, the baby becomes free (of legal entanglements) for adoption.

Public and Private Agencies

Q. As we plan for applying to adopt a child, we wonder whether there is a great difference in terms of our chances of getting a baby if we apply to a public or private agency. *Are more children available from public agencies than private ones?*

A. From the early 1950s through the mid-1970s, more children were adopted through private agencies than through public ones. That began to change in 1974, and the trend has continued ever since. There are also more independent adoptions now than there are adoptions through private agencies. This does not necessarily mean, however, that you will have a better chance of getting a baby through a public agency. Significant numbers of children available through public agencies are older, and many of that group are special-needs children.

Doubling Your Chances?

Q. Knowing how long it can take to adopt a baby, we have been wondering if there aren't ways to increase our chances of getting a baby sooner. *Is it permissible to apply to more than one adoption agency?*

A. It is permissible, but there are some good reasons not to do it. First, you may not necessarily double your chances of getting a child but only be doubling your costs, or at least increasing them. Second, the question arises about whether you should tell the agencies about the double applications. If you don't, you are violating the rule concerning the importance of being truthful, but if you do tell the truth, one or both of the agencies may feel that they don't have to work as hard for you. Finally, given the difficulty that many couples experience during the waiting period, what you may really be doubling here is the amount of stress you are under.

15

Adoption Costs

Q. My wife and I are giving serious thought to adopting a baby. We've heard a lot of conflicting information on the cost of adoption. *Are there any statistics on the average amount adoption costs in the United States?*

A. The reason you are hearing so much conflicting information is that the cost varies greatly from state to state, agency to agency, and according to the mode of adoption involved. Further detail will be offered in answer to several other questions, but there are statistics indicating that the average cost is between $5,000 and $6,000. Some situations, as when relatives adopt the child of an unwed teenager, can involve almost no costs. Black-market adoptions can soar to $50,000. There are also many adoptions that involve costs from $6,000 to $15,000—a range that is roughly equivalent to the present cost of sending a child to college for a year.

Because there are so many different routes to adoption, prospective parents can seek out the one that is best for them financially, with the understanding that higher costs usually mean less waiting time.

"Initial Service Fees"

Q. Close friends of ours registered with an adoption agency in a nearby city and plunked down $2,000 for what was called an "initial service fee." After a full year with no results, they asked for their money back. They decided it would be better to try another agency. But they were refused a refund. After that amount of time waiting, I smell a scam on the part of the adoption agency. *Are agencies within their legal rights to refuse refund of an initial service fee if they produce no results?*

A. Many adoption agencies are run as businesses and feel that their services are well worth a substantial fee, including an upfront payment. Other agencies are nonprofit, and the fees involved are far lower. The agency your friends dealt with no doubt has some fine print concerning refunds. Your friends should have been more thorough in making certain what the situation was. It should also be noted that a one-year wait is *NOT* a long one. Many adoptive parents wait two or three time as long. Thus the agency could certainly claim that it had not been given sufficient time to do the job.

Sliding-Scale Fees

Q. We have a moderate income and some savings. Since we are about to begin the adoption process, we were interested to hear that some agencies use a sliding scale in determining how large a fee is charged to adoptive parents. *How does the sliding scale work and does it affect the kind of baby you are likely to get?*

A. The sliding-scale fee system, used by many adoption agencies, simply means that people who have less money are charged less and those who are well-off are charged more. The second part of your question, however, touches on a point that has brought the sliding-scale system under attack. In 1987, for instance, the Pennsylvania Supreme Court narrowly ruled that a sliding scale was illegal. It was categorized as tantamount to "baby selling" and the court suggested that its effect was to cause white babies to be awarded primarily to well-to-do couples.

The scale has since come under fire in a number of states, although it is still in effect in most areas of the country.

Adoptions in the Big States

Q. We are residents of New York State who are trying to adopt a baby. We assume that the biggest states have the largest numbers of adoptions taking place. But we wonder if it might in fact involve waiting less time if we moved to a smaller state where adoptions are less common. *How does the size of a state's population relate to the length of time spent waiting for a child?*

A. You are getting into some false correlations here. The largest states by population are, in order, California, New York, Texas, Florida, Pennsylvania, Illinois, and Ohio, with populations ranging from 29,760,021 for California to 10,847,115 for Ohio. None of the other states has a population over 10,000,000. But the states with the most adoptions do not follow this ranking. Instead, the order is Texas, Florida, New York, Illinois, California, and Pennsylvania—Ohio has fewer adoptions than states with considerably lower population figures have.

This lack of correlation between population and the number of adoptions is one indication of the complexity of the adoption picture on a national basis. Figures on "waiting time" are not kept, and trying to make guesses about states with higher or lower population figures would be futile.

Fewer Caucasian Babies Available

Q. I recently read that the availability of adoptable Caucasian American-born infants has dropped greatly over the past two decades. *What are the social factors behind the continuing decline in the number of adoptable Caucasian children?*

A. There are three separate contributing factors. Statistics show that birth control is more widely practiced by Caucasian women than any other group. Legalized abortion is also a considerable factor. Finally, there has been a rise in the number of unmarried Caucasian women who choose to keep their babies, thanks to greatly lessened social stigma being attached to unwed mothers. (There are those, of course, who view all three of these factors as signs of the collapse of civilization.)

Where Are the Children?

Q. We've been waiting for nearly two years to adopt a child. We would like to have a baby but are willing to accept an older child. One hears constantly about children without homes, many being shipped around in the foster care system. It seems very strange to us that there are so many children without a real family home, yet so few available to be adopted. *Where are all the children?*

A. There is no question that there are large numbers of children without permanent homes. Some critics claim that many harder-to-place children are put into foster homes or institutions instead of being made available for adoption because states are paid federal funds to care for the foster children under their jurisdiction. The charge is that the welfare of many children is overlooked for monetary reasons and the maintenance of a bloated bureaucratic system. These charges are, of course, hotly denied by state agencies. It seems likely that this question will not be settled unless Congress acts to change the system, which could clearly mean a long wait.

Infants and Older Children

Q. We have been told that it is easier to adopt an older child than it is an infant, with considerably less waiting time. *Is the difference between the number of older children adopted and the number of infants adopted large enough to make it foolish to wait for an infant?*

A. Let's deal with some figures first. The latest statistical breakdown on a nationwide basis was carried out in 1986 by the National Committee for Adoption. (The federal government is notoriously uninterested in adoption figures, and they have never been part of the census.) In 1986, there were 104,088 adoptions in the United States, according to the NCA survey. Of these just over half, 50.9 percent were adoptions involving relatives of the child. Of the unrelated adoptions, 24,589 were of infants. Thus, of all adoptions, fewer than one quarter involved couples seeking an infant they were not related to. However, the difference between unrelated adoptions of infants and of older children is almost an even split. Thus, going purely by the numbers, there is no reason to give up on the idea of adopting an infant. On the other hand, there is no question you will have to wait longer for the simple reason that the demand for infants is much greater.

Special-Needs Children

Q. My husband is a physical therapist and I am a public school psychologist. We want to adopt and feel that we should put our training to use as parents of a child with special needs. But the term "special needs" seems to cover a lot of rather different kinds of children. *Exactly what causes a child to be considered as having special needs?*

A. You are correct in your observation that this term covers quite a range of situations and conditions. Deborah Burke, an official of a Massachusetts agency, defines special-needs children as "white children who are healthy and over the age of eight; groups of brothers and sisters who need to find a family together; children of color of any age; and the children whom you normally think of with special needs, be they physical, intellectual, or emotional. There are more boys than girls. The age is generally between ten and twelve."

Some may be disturbed by the inclusion here of "children of color of any age." This does not reflect racism on the part of the agencies, but is simply a recognition of the large number of non-Caucasian children without homes and the greater difficulty of placing them.

Disrupted Adoptions

Q. My son and daughter-in-law adopted a ten-year-old boy two years ago. What was meant to be a dream come true has turned into a nightmare. The boy steals, lies constantly, and shows signs of potential violence. Weekly therapy has done no good—in fact, it seems to make him worse. It breaks my heart to ask this question, *but is it possible to return an adopted child?*

A. Yes, it is possible. What are called disrupted adoptions do occur, but there will be a great deal of turmoil involved. These situations are thoroughly investigated, and the parents in the case will be considered bad risks as adoptive parents in the future regardless of how much trouble the child is causing. Some people are better prepared than others to cope with a disturbed child, and three quarters of "returned" children are placed in a new home as soon as possible.

24

Foster Parents/ Adoptive Parents

Q. My husband and I want to adopt. We are perfectly willing to take an older child, but since older children are already formed as individuals in many ways, it would be nice to be able to get to know a child better before making a final decision. We were thinking of starting out by becoming foster parents. *Are foster parents given any preference if they want to adopt a child in their care?*

A. Yes, trusted foster parents are given preference on the waiting list in most states. However, you will not become trusted if social workers get the idea that you are "auditioning" children. You will have to do your best with any children assigned to your care. Then, if that "special" child does come along, you will be in a good position to adopt.

"We Want Your Baby" Ads

Q. At first I laughed when my niece showed me a tray liner from a fast-food restaurant that read "Happily Married Couple Want to Adopt *Your* Baby" and gave a telephone number to call. Then I stopped laughing. It seemed to me that it might just as well have read "Want to Buy Your Baby." *Is this type of tasteless advertising legal?*

A. Yes, it is legal to attempt to adopt a baby in this manner. Such ads have also shown up in newspapers, on buses, and even on billboards. Bad taste is thoroughly protected by the First Amendment. You are quite right that there is an implication of baby "buying" in this kind of advertising, but at least this is better than the secretive world of shady lawyers that operates the "gray market."

Gray-Market Babies

Q. A friend of ours called recently in a state of absolute jubilation because she and her husband had just *bought a baby*, or at least that's how it sounded. It seems an unwed teenager couldn't cope with her infant daughter and basically sold the child to the highest bidder. *Is it legal to sell a baby in this way in the United States?*

A. It is illegal, but a good many such transactions occur. Some experts speak of these children as being black-market babies, but many others prefer the term "gray-market" exactly because there is, for obvious reasons, so little hard information about this kind of adoption. It really isn't known how common this situation is.

The Surrogate Mother Alternative

Q. My best friend from college, who lives in New York State and is unmarried, shocked me to death by informing me that she is carrying a baby for the infertile couple next door after being medically inseminated with the husband's sperm. *I thought this business of surrogate mothers had greatly declined since the case in 1987 involving Mary Beth Whitehead-Gould deciding to keep the baby herself, and I wonder: Why aren't legislatures putting a stop to this strange kind of arrangement?*

A. The development of surrogate mother arrangements has troubled the legal system from the start. While on the surface it may seem that such arrangements are simply a rather extreme form of "service contract," involving an infertile wife with a fertile husband and another woman willing to be artificially inseminated with the husband's sperm and to carry the fetus to term, the adoption laws eventually come into play. Regardless of what the initial contract may say, the child will not be legally regarded as belonging to the married couple unless a formal adoption takes place. If the surrogate mother balks after the child's birth, as Mary Beth Whitehead did, the courts find themselves in a legal quagmire somewhere between adoption law and divorce law.

Many state legislatures have moved to clarify the situation by attacking the financial aspects of surrogate mother arrangements. In July 1992, New York became the eighteenth state to drastically curtail this practice. Under New York law it will now be illegal to pay anything except medical expenses to the surrogate mother, and contracts between a couple and a surrogate mother will no longer have standing in state courts. Previously, fees in such situations could amount to $30,000–$40,000. At least four thousand babies have been born in the United States as a result of surrogate mothers being artificially inseminated, with about forty percent of these births occurring in New York. It can still be done, but nobody is going to make a profit out of it in New York or a growing number of other states. The practice will undoubtedly persist in an "underground" way, however.

The Adoption Option

Q. My teenage daughter has recently discovered that she is pregnant. There is much discussion in our household about whether she should have an abortion or carry the baby to term and put it up for adoption. *Are there figures on how many women take the latter course as opposed to having an abortion?*

A. Yes, there are. The most recent available figures show that the overwhelming number of women choose abortion over what is called the adoption option. Infant adoptions per thousand live births were just 15.5 children, while abortions per thousand pregnancies were 422.9 in 1986. Abortion opponents make much of such figures, but it should be noted that infant adoptions per thousand live births to unmarried women are only 28.0. Thus a great many unmarried women are keeping their babies. The problem is that many of these children end up in foster homes when they are older and much more difficult to place. Although more than 50 percent of adoptions do involve older children, welfare departments across the country are overwhelmed with the numbers of older children that are never adopted.

29

Encouraging Adoption

Q. In my not very large hometown, the unwed teenage pregnancy rate is unbelievable. I know because I am a registered nurse. When I talk to these young girls, I am appalled that 90 percent of them know absolutely nothing about the adoption process. It's either abortion or "keep my baby" for them. *Why is information about adoption so lacking at a period when we have soaring teenage pregnancy rates?*

A. One certainly can't blame these young women. Part of the problem is that the battle between antiabortion and pro-choice forces is so intense that only the extreme positions seem to make themselves heard in news stories. Both sides give lip service to the "adoption option," and some individuals try very hard to focus on it, but the message often gets lost. Another problem, often denied but very real, is that many state welfare agencies are so overwhelmed with hard-to-place children that they really would rather deal with an abortion than another potentially unplaceable child. What is really needed is the emergence of some charismatic leadership figures who can get the attention of the media on the adoption option.

Can I Stop My Daughter?

Q. My teenage daughter is unwed and pregnant and has decided to have an abortion. I am against abortion, but the argument I used with my daughter was that there are thousands of married couples who would give anything to have her baby. I begged her to carry the baby to term and put it up for adoption. But she will not listen to me. *Is there any way I can legally prevent my daughter from having an abortion and force her to put the baby up for adoption?*

A. No, there is not. A number of states have passed laws requiring parents' consent when a minor has an abortion, but the Supreme Court threw out that aspect of Pennsylvania's restrictive abortion laws at the end of the 1991–92 term, and lower courts are following suit in respect to other states that have passed such a provision. Parental notification has the Supreme Court's approval, but not parental consent.

31

A Callous Young Mother

Q. I ran into a young mother in the supermarket whom I know slightly because she and my daughter were in high school together. I asked her how her beautiful little girl was doing. She shrugged and said, "Oh, I put her up for adoption. My new boyfriend didn't like having her around. She just got in the way." The child must be two and a half years old. *Can it possibly be legal for a mother to suddenly decide to put a child of that age up for adoption?*

A. Yes, it is legal. Although not common, such sad cases do arise. Many teenage mothers quickly lose interest in a baby. Those that keep them anyway are not doing the child any favor—he or she is likely to grow up neglected or even abused. Your young mother has in fact probably done much the best thing for her child.

Birth Mothers Changing Their Minds

Q. As a couple planning to adopt, we are perturbed about stories we have heard in which the birth mother has changed her mind and taken the baby back. *How long does a birth mother have a legal right to change her mind and how often does this occur?*

A. In many states, the birth mother has a period ranging from ten to thirty days in which she can legally take the child back. About a dozen states have laws that make the adoption irrevocable as soon as the adoption papers are signed. The laws regulating how long a period the mother can have to reclaim the child are under review in numerous states, however, and it is essential to check to see what the existing law is in any given state, information that is readily available from the state branch of government that oversees health and human welfare (these government departments are differently constituted from state to state).

The greatest likelihood of a child being reclaimed occurs in the area of independent (or private) adoptions. Because independent adoption sidesteps much red tape, it also involves more potential problems. Figures are very spotty in this area, but a few investigative reports by the news media suggest that about 15 percent of birth mothers change their minds in respect to an independent adoption within the time limit. Sometimes, of course, the change of mind can come later and lead to messy court cases.

41

Birth Father Rights

Q. After I told my boyfriend that I was pregnant, he left me high and dry. Abortion is out of the question, so I am going to put the baby up for adoption. Considering the circumstances, I feel the baby is mine to do with as I choose. But I worry about my boyfriend making trouble for me and the baby in the future. *Does my ex-boyfriend have any legal rights to the child?*

A. The legal rights of the birth father are a complicated issue— largely because the law tends to be vague and even contradictory here. And, of course, these laws vary from state to state. In your case, it might be that his unwillingness to help you means that his rights are void. However, if his name appears on the birth certificate, he could go so far as to block adoption proceedings. To prevent this from happening, some unwed mothers don't reveal the name of the father.

Medicaid Help for Pregnant Teens?

Q. I am an unwed pregnant teenager who has no choice but to put my baby up for adoption. *Can a pregnant teenager get any financial help from Medicaid?*

A. The federal government has mandated that Medicaid be available to first-time pregnant women. But the number of obstetricians and gynecologists who accept Medicaid are regrettably few. Many unwed pregnant women refuse to make use of the welfare system out of pride, but this is the obvious option. Such aid is always available from public adoption agencies, which are part of the welfare system. Private agencies will provide funds to the pregnant mother that are covered by the adoption fees they charge to prospective adoptive parents.

No Permanent Home

Q. I decided months ago to put my baby, due in about six weeks, up for adoption. But now I am worried. A young woman I recently met was put up for adoption when she was four. She has told me terrible stories of never being permanently placed with one family. Instead she was shuttled from one foster home to another. I don't want this to happen to my baby. *Is it usual for babies to be placed with foster families before they are adopted?*

A. Most adoptive couples want an infant. Since the demand for babies is greater than the number available, you can be quite certain that your baby will find a permanent home very quickly. Unfortunately, what happened to your friend is not uncommon. Many children four years and older are difficult to place. It is dreadful to think that a child could feel "over the hill" at the age of five or nine, but many do have that sense in their chances for adoption. Experts agree that most foster parents are kind and caring, but problems do arise, and there are children who go through a very difficult time, being moved from family to family. Too often, a child who has moved a lot develops a number of psychological problems that can lead to being moved around even more.

Relinquishment Before Birth?

Q. I plan to put my unborn baby up for adoption. I don't even want to see it because I hate the man who got me pregnant. *Is it possible to legally relinquish my birth mother rights even before the baby arrives?*

A. No state will allow relinquishment before birth. This is because even women like yourself who want nothing to do with the baby have been known to change their minds after the baby is born. If you really do not wish to even see the baby, however, that can usually be arranged.

Private Agency Acceptance

Q. We are an "upper-middle-class" couple with three children. Two of them are terrific kids, but the youngest has always been a problem. She has a history of drug use and is now pregnant out of wedlock. *Will our daughter's history of drug use make it more difficult to place the baby for adoption through a private agency?*

A. Very likely. Public agencies have to deal with anyone who shows up on their doorstep. Private agencies do not, and by their very nature want to be able to assure their clients that any child in their hands is in good health and comes from a fairly stable birth mother. It is that assurance, in part, that their clients are willing to pay for. Thus your daughter will probably have to seek help from a public agency.

The Right Way to Say It

Q. My favorite niece and her husband are trying to adopt a baby. I'm very supportive of the idea, and I know that it's important to be careful about the kind of terminology one uses in speaking about adoption. I don't want to put my foot in my mouth. *What are some of the correct usages in talking about adoption?*

A. An excellent rundown of correct usage was put together by Marietta Spencer, director of postlegal adoption services at the Children's Society of Minnesota. She contrasts the right and wrong way to talk about a number of adoption concerns:

Don't say: Giving away your child.
Do say: Making an adoption plan.

Don't say: Real mother or natural mother.
Do say: Birth mother or biological mother.

Don't say: Illegitimate child.
Do say: Child of unmarried parents.

Don't say: Not the real parents.
Do say: Adoptive parents.

A Case of Nerves

Q. I am not normally a nervous person, but I just blew my first interview at the adoption agency. I couldn't stop shaking and was near tears by the time it was over. On the basis of that interview, I don't think anyone would choose me to be a mother if I were the last person on earth. *Does someone who is so nervous at a first interview have a prayer to rebound as the process continues?*

A. Of course. Most adoption social workers are used to nervousness and are sympathetic with applicants. That's why decisions aren't made just on the basis of one interview. Now that you've gotten over the first hurdle, you would be wise to do some home rehearsing, with a friend asking questions. But don't try to memorize answers—it is also important to be yourself and to answer spontaneously.

Overemphasizing Infertility

Q. My niece gave me a long account of her first interview with an adoption agency caseworker. (Her husband was there, too, but it seems that she did most of the talking.) She seemed very pleased with herself about how things had gone, but it sounds to me as though she spent far too much time talking about the fact that her infertility made adoption her only remaining chance to be a mother. There was a "last-resort" tone that crept into her account that I found unattractive. *Are adoption agency caseworkers likely to pick up on the idea that someone wouldn't be applying unless it was a matter of desperation, or are they used to this kind of attitude?*

A. They are very likely to pick up on the "hidden message" that your niece doesn't fundamentally approve of adoption and is simply desperate, and they will not like it. They do, of course, hear quite a lot of this kind of thing, but they are going to be much better disposed to someone who talks about knowing adopted children and adoptive parents and that as a result, it seemed a natural course to pursue when it was discovered that biological children were out of the question.

Home Owners and Apartment Renters

Q. We rent a large sunny apartment in a good area, but are concerned that adoption agencies might frown on a couple who do not own their own house. *Is it important to be a home owner in order to adopt a child?*

A. No. Whether you check the *rent* or *own* box on a loan application to a financial institution can make a big difference. But it is of no importance to adoption agencies. There are many people, especially in cities, who rent apartments but have much more disposable income than a couple with a new house in the suburbs. Agencies look at the overall financial picture and how the couple makes use of their income.

Uncle Harry Lives
with Us Too

Q. After five years of my failing to conceive, we have decided to adopt. We believe ourselves well qualified to be good parents but there is one possible problem. My husband's uncle Harry, who is a semi-invalid, has lived with us for two years. He is in no way an undue burden and we love him dearly. *How would an adoption agency feel about the presence of a relative in our home?*

A. Uncle Harry could be a plus or a minus in the eyes of an agency. On the one hand, the fact that you have opened your home to a relative in need will undoubtedly speak well for you as caring people. But it might seem that you already have your hands full. You should be prepared for some close questioning about exactly how much care Uncle Harry requires and what his financial situation is.

The Objecting Grandparent

Q. My husband comes from a distinguished old family with a great deal of money. I have been unable to conceive (it turns out we both have reproductive problems) and we decided to adopt. My husband's parents were enraged and said that if we went ahead my husband would be disinherited. They already have other grandchildren. We are going ahead anyway, hoping they will eventually come around. *How common is it for the prospective grandparents of an adopted child to reject the whole idea?*

A. It is more common than generally realized. A study by sociologist David Kirk puts the number at 20 percent. The reasons given may be religious, social ("what would my friends say?"), a concern for "bloodlines," or altogether irrational. Some prospective grandparents have even been known to contact the agency and try to derail the process. But while agencies do value family ties, most are unlikely to decide against you on this point, especially if the other set of grandparents is supportive. In your case, your husband's decision to ignore threats of disinheritance would probably garner him high marks in terms of character.

Career-Minded Mother

Q. My husband and I had our first interview with an adoption agency recently. All went well until I said that I planned to continue my nine-to-five job after the placement, but that my mother, who lives next door, would care for the child during the day. The social worker turned pale. Believe me, no baby could have better care than my mother is capable of giving. *Do all agencies frown on a situation in which the adoptive mother continues to work?*

A. Most agencies favor a full-time, stay-at-home mother for at least the first year. There are many studies that indicate how important the early months of a baby's life are to the development of a well-adjusted child. But with so many women working full-time, attitudes are beginning to change on this subject. The social worker you were dealing with may be very conservative on this issue. Another might see the presence of your mother as a good basis for compromise in your case. Certainly family ties are regarded as important to the upbringing of any child.

When There Is Already a Biological Child

Q. I gave birth to a daughter after an extremely difficult pregnancy—so difficult that I was strongly advised by my physician not to have another child. But both my husband and myself were "only" children and feel that it was sometimes a lonely way to grow up. We want to adopt a brother or sister for the sake of our daughter, and of course for our own joy. *Are adoption agencies likely to put us at the bottom of the list since we already have a biological child?*

A. In your case there should be no problem at all in this regard. While agencies prefer that the prospective parents have no more than one child already, or none at all, it is widely agreed that it is healthy for an adopted baby to have a sibling, either a preexisting one or one to be adopted later.

Adopting in Your Forties

Q. My husband and I are both forty-three. We now have the time, maturity, and financial stability to be fine parents, at least as we see it. *Would agencies think that we are too old to adopt a child since we are over forty?*

A. Most agencies prefer that the parents be no more than forty years older than the child they adopt. And an agency will want to ensure as far as possible that a child will have a long relationship with the adoptive parents, at least through college. But exceptions are made in this regard. The essential factor in such cases is that the adoptive parents both be in excellent health. A history of early heart attacks in the family of either parent, or even the existence of high blood pressure in one of them could work against being given the chance to adopt.

Too Highbrow a Lifestyle

Q. An adoption agency has just rejected us as potential parents for a baby boy. In terms of health, financial stability, and many other factors we met the criteria with no problem. The sympathetic social worker we had been dealing with told us that although she herself thought we would be fine parents, her superiors had decided that we had a highbrow lifestyle that was not appropriate to bringing up a boy. In other words, we go to the opera and the ballet and have little interest in baseball, football, and other "manly" sports, although we do enjoy tennis, golf, and figure skating. *Is it really legitimate to turn down prospective parents because they don't go to Dodgers games?*

A. Your situation is not too common, but such problems do crop up at some agencies. Legitimate or not, people do get turned down occasionally because they are not regarded as sufficiently "all-American." Most agencies are not this narrow-minded, however. Start over again with another agency, and when asked about your interests try to work opera and golf into the same sentence so that you come off as "well-rounded." If you say, "Well, we love opera and grand-slam tennis," it gives a very different impression than if you go on about the opera and ballet, and your enjoyment of tennis comes out only as an answer to a specific question.

Suburban Bias?

Q. We have been on the waiting list with a private adoption agency for nearly two years. We own a large co-op in New York City, but we get the feeling that the very fact that we are big-city residents is operating against us. *Do agencies tend to have a bias against city dwellers as adoptive parents?*

A. Some agencies do clearly prefer a couple who lives in suburbia, complete with the picket fence. Since you have been waiting so long already, it hardly makes sense to change adoption agencies at this point, essentially starting all over again.

Try bringing up this matter directly with the agency, but don't do it in a hostile way. If you have parents or relatives who live in nonurban areas, or have summer homes, make it clear that your child would certainly get to visit them and gain experience of that kind of living.

Couples with Troubled Marriages

Q. We have been married for seven years but have separated twice. My wife and I now feel that our troubles are behind us and we would like to adopt a baby. *Do past marital problems make it more difficult to adopt a child?*

A. Yes. You are likely to be considered high-risk candidates as adoptive parents. Adoption agencies look above all for stability in prospective parents. They are likely to have a lot of questions about your assertion that things are now all right. If you have undergone therapy as a couple, they might want to have your permission to talk to the therapist. One of their major concerns will be whether you are seeking to adopt a child in order to save your marriage. That is a situation agencies want to avoid at all costs.

A Recovering Alcoholic

Q. I am a recovering alcoholic who has not had a drink in nine years. It wasn't easy, of course, but for that very reason I feel that my long record of abstinence should be a point in my favor. At the same time I understand many people would not see it that way. *Will my alcoholic past put an end to my and my wife's dreams of being a family of three?*

A. There are no hard-and-fast rules here. Attitudes are likely to vary from agency to agency and even from caseworker to caseworker. Just the words "recovering alcoholic" scare many people. There are likely to be fears that the stress of being a parent could knock you off the wagon again. But the fact that you have been dry for so long may help you a good deal. It will be essential to be utterly truthful about the situation. You will certainly have a difficult time trying to adopt, but it is not out of the question that you could succeed.

College Indiscretions

Q. My wife and I both toyed with marijuana while in college, as did most of our friends. That was fifteen years ago and now we don't even smoke cigarettes. We are planning an adoption but are a bit worried about confessing our past use of marijuana. *Could mild drug use fifteen years ago derail our attempt to adopt a baby?*

A. Not necessarily. A verbal admission of smoking marijuana in college does not give you a criminal record. In fact, your honesty might even be commended. Your tone could be important though. Don't report this information in a lighthearted way.

Living Together Before Marriage

Q. My husband and I have been married for only two and a half years, but we lived together for three years before the wedding. *Does the fact that a couple lived together before marrying count as a plus or a minus in the view of adoption agencies?*

A. In the old days (only a couple of decades ago in our fast-moving world) cohabitation before marriage was quite often considered a minus. But that kind of arrangement has become so common that the pendulum has swung in the other direction. Most agencies prefer that a couple have been married for at least two years, and these days regard the fact that they lived together before that as a plus. It should be noted, however, that some recent studies have shown that couples who do not live together before marriage have lower divorce rates. Since the reasons why this should be the case are very murky, it is not likely that these studies will have any immediate effect, but down the line they may cause another shift in attitudes.

Unmarried Adoptive Parents?

Q. We are a couple who have been living together for seven happy and fulfilling years, with only one omission: We cannot produce a child. We firmly believe that getting married is just a matter of acquiring a meaningless piece of paper, and we don't intend to change our views. *What are our chances as an unmarried couple of adopting a baby?*

A. Your chances are nil. Adoption agencies think that piece of paper means a great deal. It came to light during the scandal that erupted around Woody Allen and Mia Farrow that Allen had in fact been allowed to adopt two children that had previously been adopted by Farrow, despite the fact that they weren't married. Adoption lawyers believe it was the first time that had happened in the United States, and the uproar that resulted when Allen and Farrow split makes it doubly certain that adoptions by unmarried couples are going to remain out of the question.

Transracial Adoption

Q. My wife and I have been on the waiting list to adopt a black baby for over two years. As far as we can see, the only problem is that we are white. We both grew up in racially mixed neighborhoods and have many black friends. And clearly there are a great many black children in need of homes. But it seems to us that we are having doors slammed in our faces because we are white. *Is it legal for an agency to block an adoption because we are white and the baby would be black?*

A. No, it is not legal. But transracial adoption has been fraught with controversy for many years. The common practice by agencies is to place children with parents of the same racial background. You are quite right, however, that there are many black children in need of homes. Unfortunately, a degree of reverse discrimination often enters the picture. For example, the National Association of Black Social Workers feels strongly that placing a black child with a white couple might rob him of his African-American heritage. Statistics show, however, that about 70 percent of transracial adoptions are fully successful.

A Mixed-Race Couple

Q. My wonderful wife is black and I am white. The fact that we have an interracial marriage seems to give the adoption agency we are dealing with major, although largely unadmitted, problems. We have not made any requirement that the baby be of a particular race. In fact, as Sammy Davis, Jr., once said about the baby his Swedish wife, May Britt, was carrying, "I don't care if it's polka-dot." But I think maybe the agency really regards *us* as polka-dot. *Can adoption agencies really get away with this racist attitude?*

A. No, not openly. But as Fred Powledge points out in *The New Adoption Maze*, many agencies look askance at couples who don't fit certain stereotypes. They're looking for prospective parents who are not only married, but are of "identical skin color and relatively young; the husband is the breadwinner and the wife doesn't work outside the home; the couple practices a religion, it's the same religion for both of them and it is one of the *brand-name* religions." This kind of stereotype is less and less typical of the real America, but even if the likes of Dan Quayle haven't realized that fact, some adoption agencies have. You need to look for an agency where the personnel is willing to talk about these issues right up front rather than dodging and weaving.

Black Prospective Parents/ White Caseworker

Q. We are a black couple, married for five years, trying to adopt a black baby. Our caseworker is white, and we feel that the whole torturous process would move faster if we had a black caseworker. *Why don't agencies automatically assign prospective parents a caseworker of the same race?*

A. Because that in itself would be discriminatory. Some black couples have charged white caseworkers with being racist, but it is rare. Individuals with racist attitudes are unlikely to be drawn to social work in the first place, and would likely be weeded out quite quickly. It is understandable that you might feel more comfortable with a black caseworker, but it is doubtful that the adoption process is proceeding more slowly because your caseworker is white. Prospective parents of all races complain endlessly about how long the process takes.

Of Different Faiths?

Q. Although we are churchgoing people, it makes no difference to us in adopting a child what the religious background of the birth mother might be. *How important is the religious background of adoptive parents to agencies?*

A. Religion can be a major issue or a very minor one, depending on circumstances. Agencies affiliated with a particular church are of course going to seek out adoptive parents of that religion. It can also be a serious matter of concern for the birth mother in some open adoptions. Many private and even public agencies will take the birth mother's wishes into account on the matter, but since the files will be sealed in a traditional adoption situation, the agency is in no way duty-bound to follow through to the detriment of placing the child in the best possible adoptive home.

Discrimination Against
Single Mothers?

Q. I have been told by several sources that my chances of adopting a baby are very slim because I am single. This disturbs me because I have all the qualifications to be a loving and caring parent except for one: a husband. I was in large part responsible for raising my younger brother and sister after our mother died of cancer. As I am single by choice, it seems discriminatory to rule me out as a potentially fine mother. *Is it legal for an adoption agency to deny a single woman the right to adopt?*

A. No, it's not legal, but that really isn't the point here. Most agencies have a waiting list of fifty to a hundred couples for every adoptable baby. A single applicant is inevitably at a disadvantage given these numbers. The fact that you have extensive "mothering" experience is a definite plus, but if you give the impression that you have a chip on your shoulder about "discriminatory" practices you will cancel out that advantage in a hurry.

Single Male Father

Q. I am a thirty-eight-year-old single male who very much wants to adopt a child. I lost my wife to cancer two years ago. Because I run my own consulting business out of my house, I wouldn't have to rely on day care. *What are the chances of a single male adopting a child?*

A. Adoption by a single male parent is more common than it used to be. No state agency in the country can forbid adoption by a single parent, male or female. Once you have applied to an agency and it has carried out its home study procedures, you will be eligible to adopt. However, the waiting period will almost certainly be longer than for two-parent applicants.

Lesbian Moms

Q. My daughter, who lives in Florida, has been denied the right to apply to adopt a child because she is a lesbian. *Is it really legal to totally exclude someone from adopting because of sexual preference?*

A. In your daughter's case, yes. Florida and New Hampshire are the only two states that ban adoption by homosexuals outright, although the process can be very difficult even in states where such bans do not exist.

Florida is so strict about dealing with homosexual parents that in 1992 a lesbian couple in Tampa had their six-year-old foster child, a boy, taken away from them because they lived together. Homosexuals and lesbians can serve as foster parents, but not in situations where they live under the same roof as a couple. "We were his moms," the couple said. But they would have had to live apart from each other in order to keep the child they wanted to care for—a fine example of catch-22 logic.

Picture Perfect

Q. Looking at photographs at our adoption agency, we saw the child of our dreams. He is picture perfect. But there seems to be a problem. The boy has an older sister who is also up for adoption, and the agency says they cannot be separated. We do not want to take on two children at once. The situation smacks of "buy one, get one free" to us. *Does the agency have the right to deny us our special choice unless we take the sister too?*

A. Although there are many "picture perfect" children waiting to be adopted, most agencies agree that separating siblings is a very bad idea. Also, keep in mind the old truism that you don't judge a book by its cover. The prettiest children, biological or adopted, sometimes have more problems growing up into well-balanced adults.

The Word "Pity" Is a Problem

Q. We knew when we were married that we would have to adopt if we wanted children, and we now feel we are ready to take that step. We see so many magazine articles and television news features on unwanted special-needs children, and they fill our hearts with pity. We feel we could give a good home to a special-needs child. *We know several people who have waited a very long time before a child was found for them and wonder if things go more quickly for those who adopt a handicapped child?*

A. Yes, it is usually "quicker" to adopt a handicapped child because there are so many in need of homes. But you will be screened even more thoroughly than most would-be adoptive parents to make certain that you are fully prepared to cope with a handicapped or troubled child. Many people who think they would be good parents to such a child really do not have the right temperament. And, however good your intentions, many adoption agencies would take your use of the word "pity" as a warning sign. Not only should no child be adopted out of pity, any child that has serious problems is going to require parents chock-full of patience, resourcefulness, and love and who recognize that pity stands in the way of helping a child to become more successful at developing as a self-reliant person.

Good Intentions, But . . .

Q. The more I read and see on television, the sorrier I feel for all the orphans in the world. Although we have two children of our own, we would be more than willing to help out by adopting at least one child from a devastated foreign country. *How much red tape is involved in adopting a foreign orphan?*

A. There is a great deal of red tape involved. But you really should rethink your motives to adopt, anyway. Your intentions are kind, but to "help out" is not regarded as a good reason to adopt. Consider making a contribution to one or more of the several charitable organizations that help to support and educate orphaned children in their own countries around the world.

Fear of Crib Death

Q. Our four-month-old son was a victim of crib death ten months ago. My wife is so afraid of going through the same thing again that we decided to try to adopt a slightly older child, say, one to two years of age. Adoption agencies do not seem to want to give us the time of day. *Are we going to be forever marked as unfit parents because our son was a victim of crib death?*

A. The way in which your son died is not the problem here. While crib death is still not fully understood in medical terms, it is certainly recognized, especially by professionals, that crib death in no way indicates neglect by the parents. What undoubtedly does trouble the agencies you have talked to is that you and particularly your wife are still very strongly affected by the death of your son, still in mourning. The very fact that your wife wants to adopt an older child for fear of a recurrence of your tragedy would make it clear that you are not yet ready to deal with another child, whether biological or adopted. It will take time and quite possibly therapy before you and your wife reach the point of being seriously considered as adoptive parents.

☐☐☐☐☐ **65** ☐☐☐☐☐

A Damaged Ego

Q. After extensive medical tests, we finally know that my husband is infertile. We had previously agreed we would adopt if either of us proved to be infertile, but he now gets very upset when I bring the subject up. It could obviously have been the case that *I* was infertile; in fact I had prepared myself for that possibility. *Do men usually take the news that they are infertile worse than women do?*

A. Infertility of husband, wife, or both partners, is the largest single cause for couples deciding to adopt. Many couples who eventually adopt, however, go through a rocky period when the identity of the infertile partner is fully established. Individuals of both sexes sometimes take the news that they are infertile very badly. But the reaction can be particularly severe among men who confuse "fertility" with "virility." An infertile man can have just as active and fulfilling a sex life as one who is fertile, it is just that his body does not produce enough sperm to lead to conception.

Far more men are infertile than is generally recognized. What's more, there are indications that the rate is rising. Two studies at colleges in Florida and Texas in the late 1980s produced results that alarmed scientists—the rate among those young men at their sexual peak was around 25 percent. There are many experts who believe that environmental pollution is the culprit and that the rates of infertility will continue to climb. Your husband has plenty of company, but it sounds as though he may need therapy to help him deal with what he has discovered—and before any attempt is made to adopt a child.

74

66

A Sudden Widow

Q. My daughter and son-in-law were well along in the adoption process when tragedy struck. My son-in-law died of an utterly unexpected heart attack at the age of thirty-five. My daughter very much wants to go through with adopting the baby, but so far she has not informed the agency of his death, which occurred a month ago. I should add that she was left very well off financially. *Does a young widow who was already involved in the adoption process with her husband have a chance to be approved in light of her changed circumstances?*

A. Yes, but she will have to be completely reevaluated in terms of being a single mother. It is vital that she inform the agency immediately of the death of her husband and request a reevaluation. The major question that will concern them is your daughter's emotional health. If it appears that her continued interest in adopting a baby is primarily a matter of filling a sudden vacuum in her life, the agency is likely to take a wait-and-see attitude. Eventual adoption is certainly not precluded, but she must recognize the fact that she will be to a large extent starting over from scratch. In her favor will be the fact that she is already a known quantity to the agency. Patience will be required.

░░░░░░ **67** ░░░░░░

Suddenly Pregnant

Q. After five years of marriage my husband and I are still child-less. We have been on an adoption agency waiting list for eleven months. At the same time, we have continued to spend thousands of dollars on infertility services. *If I should in fact become pregnant and still wanted to adopt as well, would that be permitted?*

A. Some agencies might feel that dealing with two infants at once would not be a very good idea. A lot would depend on the timing of the birth of your biological child. There might be some concern that having two children almost the same age, one biological and one adopted, could have an adverse effect on the adopted child. The adoption agency might therefore put you lower down on the waiting list.

Loneliness Is Not Enough

Q. I am a thirty-five-year-old widow. My husband was killed in a plane crash two years ago. He left me well taken care of financially, but I am very lonely. I have daydreams about adopting a baby girl. *How would an adoption agency feel about a widow wanting to adopt?*

A. You would be treated as a single parent. However, adoption agencies do not look on loneliness as a good reason to adopt a child and would probably balk at your request to be considered. One of the most important criteria for adoptive parents, from the point of view of agencies, is that they be stable, well-adjusted people with focused lives.

Whose Baby Is It Anyway?

Q. Since my wife and I first applied to adopt ten months ago, I lost my job in the reorganization following the merger of the company I worked for with a larger one. We get the strong feeling that the adoption agency is stalling us at this juncture. My wife's parents, who are very wealthy, are helping to support us until I can find another position, and they are also more than willing to pay for any and all expenses involved in the adoption. *Can an agency block an adoption because the father is unemployed when there are sufficient funds available anyway?*

A. Most agencies consider an unemployed husband as perhaps not sufficiently responsible for fatherhood, regardless of the resources available to the couple. But special circumstances might make them more amenable to the situation. In your situation, you may be judged the victim of the economy. And wealthy in-laws can't hurt—money talks with some adoption agencies. But the fact that your in-laws would be paying for the adoption in toto may give them pause, leading them to ask "Whose baby is this, anyway?" There are a lot of variables in this kind of situation, but an agency would probably be happier if you got a new job, even if it paid considerably less than your previous position.

Loss of the Sex Drive

Q. Our lives have become so consumed by the quest to adopt a baby that we don't even have sex anymore. *If a couple's sexual relationship has been put on the back burner during the adoption process does it mean they should reconsider adoption?*

A. Couples whose sexual relationship has disintegrated during the adoption process need to get their own lives in order before attempting to bring a third person into their lives. It is very important to reestablish your own loving union before adopting, with the help of a therapist if necessary. It is not uncommon for couples to experience sexual problems after the birth of a biological child. That can easily undermine a marriage. The fact that you are having trouble at this stage is not a good sign.

Pre-Adoption Counseling

Q. What is all this talk about receiving counseling before adopting a baby? When my husband and I went to the initial interview, I made it quite clear that I had practically raised my little brothers. "Yes, I know how to change a diaper, and it never bothered me at all." I don't need counseling on the care of babies. *Do all adoptive parents have to go through counseling, regardless of their background experience?*

A. Yes, and with good reason. Many experts in child care feel that the great majority of biological parents ought to receive counseling, but the fact that it can't be required means that large numbers of parents run into serious problems. Too often they only get outside help after signs of abuse come to the attention of authorities. Adoption agencies are in a position to require counseling, and it is in the best interests of all concerned. Keep in mind that knowing how to change a diaper is the very least of it in being a good parent.

A Place to Find Guidance

Q. We are frustrated beyond words with the "it depends" answers and the endless jargon we get from our adoption agency. A number of books have been helpful to us, but what we really need is to be able to talk to people who have been through the adoption process. *We have heard about meetings held for parents who have recently adopted a child, and we wonder if a couple who is just beginning the process would be welcome at such gatherings?*

A. Absolutely! By all means take advantage of this resource. Groups exist in innumerable localities, large and small, across the country. Their particular purpose is for new adoptive parents to discuss problems they have run into, as well as to share their joy. These groups warmly welcome those who are just starting out on the path they have successfully followed to a happy conclusion. You will find that the experience of these people who have "been through the mill" is immensely helpful, even if you sometimes get conflicting advice. Going to meetings can give you real insight into how the process works.

The Home Study

Q. In preparing ourselves to apply for the right to adopt, we have done a lot of reading, but we find the material we have seen on the term "home study" unclear. Just the words make us uneasy. *Exactly what does a home study consist of?*

A. Some people do find the term "home study" threatening, but it is nothing to get unduly anxious about. Here's how it works. A caseworker from the agency you apply to will come to your house to evaluate your lifestyle. They are professionals whose only concern is the welfare of the adopted child.

Your house should be clean and neat, but don't race around redecorating or trying to turn your house into something very different from what it normally is. Caseworkers are very quick to pick up on the presentation of a "false front," and that will definitely work against you.

Dogs and Children

Q. The caseworker assigned to our home study was taken aback when she saw our two dogs on her first visit to our house, even though it had been made clear from the start that we did have dogs. Perhaps the problem was that they are very large dogs, but as any dog expert will tell you, larger dogs are the very best with young children. We tried to explain all this and told her that children in the neighborhood played with our dogs all the time. Her only response was to tell horror stories about the number of babies harmed by household pets. *Can an adoption agency reject our application because we have dogs?*

A. This is a question that comes up quite frequently. Some agencies find that people who have pets make better parents, since caring for a pet involves many kinds of responsibility and a loving nature. Other agencies and caseworkers tend to dwell on the horror stories. It could be that your caseworker simply doesn't like dogs, in which case you might want to consider asking for a different person.

▯:▯:▯:▯:▯ **75** ▯:▯:▯:▯:▯

Questioning Next-door Neighbors

Q. Our next-door neighbors are trying to adopt a baby. We don't
know them well, but they are pleasant people and good neighbors.
I was quite astonished recently when a social worker from an
adoption agency rang my front doorbell and proceeded to ask all
kinds of questions about our neighbors' lifestyle. Did they have
any bad habits, did they fight or have loud parties, that sort of
thing. I said simply that they seemed like fine people. *Is it legal for
a social worker from an adoption agency to bother neighbors with
all kinds of prying questions?*

A. It's just as legal as selling magazines or makeup door-to-door.
You don't have to buy the makeup or answer the social worker's
questions. Many people hesitate to turn a social worker away,
however, for fear of that being seen as a negative reflection on the
couple being investigated. Social workers are trained professionals
trying to do a job. Your response was perfectly appropriate.

Sex Questions Are Out of Bounds

Q. My husband and I are furious! Our caseworker had asked every question under the sun about our past, present, and future lives. We gladly obliged with detailed answers. But then she started asking intimate questions about our sex habits. For instance, "Do you practice birth control?" Of course we don't practice birth control—I've been trying to conceive for five years. She also asked how often we have sex and even whether my husband wore Jockey shorts, saying they could cause sterility. *Is it normal for a caseworker to delve into every nook and cranny of the sex lives of adoption applicants?*

A. No, it is not normal. Your caseworker was way out of bounds. This is a situation that should be reported to the higher-ups at the particular agency.

Income Tax Returns

Q. Since we are both self-employed—one of us is a writer and the other is an interior decorator—we file separate income tax forms. They are extremely complicated and not easy to grasp (our accountant says they are a nightmare). As prospective adoptive parents, we worry that agencies will not know what to make of them. *Do adoption agencies insist upon seeing past tax returns of couples applying to adopt?*

A. Not always. For example if you have a titled position—say, Assistant Vice President—with a major firm, tax returns would probably not be necessary. On the other hand, if you have changed jobs several times over the years, an agency is likely to require income tax forms. Self-employed couples like you are almost certain to be asked to provide this information. Don't just turn them over, however. Insist upon going through them with agency personnel so that you can explain any misconceptions that may arise. Most self-employed people, especially in the arts, have incomes that vary considerably from year to year. But keep in mind that adoption agencies are more interested in how you *manage* what you make than they are in how much you make.

Why Fingerprinting?

Q. I thought I was being joshed when a friend told me that she and her husband had been fingerprinted in one of the many steps toward adopting a child. She was *not* joking. *Is fingerprinting the norm in the adoption process?*

A. It isn't the norm, but it is being integrated into the process more and more. The reason for fingerprinting is to make sure that prospective adoptive parents are not felons. It should be noted that fingerprinting is becoming more common throughout American society, from corporations to public schools. It is often presented as a protective measure; for instance, school systems that have advocated fingerprinting (on a voluntary basis) point out that if a child were kidnapped, having his or her fingerprints on file would put the police a step ahead of the kidnapper. There's no question that law enforcement agencies would like to see the day when everyone is routinely fingerprinted, but there are those who regard this as an invasion of privacy and will fight it every step of the way. No one planning to adopt in the coming years should be surprised to be asked to supply his or her fingerprints.

Offensive Jargon

Q. My daughter and her husband are being interviewed by an adoption agency. Several times a question came up about who would be the "prime caretaker" of the child. That upset my daughter. She will, after all, be an adoptive mother, not somebody who looks after a building while the owners are away! *Are we out of line to find the term "caretaker" offensive?*

A. You and your daughter have reason to be upset. The term "caretaker" is an example of sociological jargon that gets used without people thinking through the implications. Some agencies fail to properly educate their caseworkers about terms to avoid in the interest of tact. All the term really means is "who will be at home to care for the baby on a day-to-day basis?" There are, of course, husbands who work at home and care for the child during the day while the wife works.

Changing Social Workers

Q. The social worker assigned to us as we attempt to adopt a baby has been rude and hostile. For example, in the course of her home study, she spotted a coffee cup in the kitchen sink and clutched at her chest as though she was about to faint. "Clean kitchens are very important," she said. "Dirty houses are not a good environment for a child to grow up in." May I say, with pride, that I keep a pristine house. That woman could eat off my kitchen floor so long as she didn't mind a slight Spic and Span℠ aftertaste. *Can we request a different social worker from the agency?*

A. Absolutely. You have a *right* to do so. Agencies are aware that personality conflicts sometimes crop up between social workers and prospective clients. You should be prepared to deal with some more red tape in the course of making the change, however.

Unexplained Rejections

Q. I am furious. My son and daughter-in-law have received a polite but firm rejection of their application to become adoptive parents. This makes no sense to me whatever. They are normal, all-American people with financial stability. *Can an adoption agency turn a couple down for no apparent reason?*

A. It may be that your perspective concerning your son and daughter-in-law is not realistic. But it could also be that the agency was too picky. This does happen sometimes. Have your son and daughter-in-law demand a full explanation from the agency as to why they were turned down. *That is their right.* At the least, they will have a better idea about how to strengthen their presentation to another agency if they have a full understanding of what went wrong on this first try.

A Lawyer Comes Later

Q. We are seriously contemplating trying to adopt a foreign child. Obviously there are many things to learn, including the policies of the U.S. Immigration and Naturalization Service concerning adopted children. *Should we start out by hiring a lawyer who specializes in immigration?*

A. No, you don't need a lawyer to get your hands on government pamphlets. Go to your local library and ask for help at the reference desk. The library will have a catalogue of the Government Printing Office publications, with price listings, which are very modest. Write for any pamphlets that might apply and read them thoroughly. Then, when it comes time down the line to deal with a lawyer, you will have a much better idea of the questions to ask him and will be able to understand his answers more easily.

░░░░░ **83** ░░░░░

South Korean Adoptions

Q. We had read that more children from South Korea were adopted in the United States than from any other country. This led us to believe that it must therefore be fairly easy to adopt a Korean child. We now find that it is very difficult. *Since South Korea does allow many foreign adoptions, why is the process made so difficult?*

A. No foreign adoptions are easy, but South Korea does have particularly tough standards. The number of children the country allows to be adopted abroad is not really in contradiction to the tight rules that apply, however. For both economic reasons and the small size of most Korean homes, it is very difficult for a South Korean family to raise more than two children. There is also a considerable stigma attached to children of unwed mothers, especially if they are racially mixed. Ancestor worship requires both racial purity and a child sanctioned by marriage. Yet, at the same time, South Koreans greatly cherish children—in a complex way that is difficult for many Americans to grasp—and agencies want to see to it that a child adopted by foreigners gets the very best parents possible. South Korean agencies thus run very tight ships indeed. A couple chosen to adopt a South Korean child has passed a test of worthiness that makes them quite special people.

Sharing a Bedroom

Q. We have two sons of our own, ages eight and ten. They are very socially aware kids, and as a family we have talked about the possibility of adopting another boy around their ages, perhaps a child who has lost his parents in the turmoil surrounding the breakup of the Soviet Union. The boys have their own bedrooms, but either one would be willing to share his bedroom with an adopted brother. *Would an adoption agency frown on the idea of the adopted boy sharing a bedroom with one of our sons?*

A. Many agencies would see that as a plus with an older child. Sharing a bedroom with one of your sons would in the view of adoption caseworkers help the newcomer to feel more a part of the family from the start, rather than just a visitor. If you did adopt a foreign child, this kind of arrangement would also hasten the development of his English-language skills.

The Strange Case
of Minnesota

Q. Having lived in several different countries around the world, we feel we would be particularly suitable parents for an adopted foreign child. An old friend who lives in Minnesota tells us we should move there, since adoptions of foreign-born children are so common. This seems to us quite odd. *Is it really true that Minnesota has a great many adoptions of foreign-born children?*

A. Yes, it is true, and it is also in some ways odd. The state has one of the lowest percentages of adoptions of unrelated children, and by far the highest percentage of adoptions of foreign-born children except for Hawaii. The reason is that Minnesota laws facilitate the adoption of foreign children—which helps to balance out the state's tradition of relatives adopting unwanted or orphaned children. But there are twenty-two states in which more than 20 percent of unrelated adopted children are foreign-born, so there is no particular need to move to Minnesota.

Native-American Adoptees

Q. I have some Cherokee blood on my mother's side, and my husband and I are wondering about the possibility of adopting a Native-American child, since it is clear that many of them are in foster care. *How difficult is it to adopt a Native-American child?*

A. There are many difficulties involved. The Indian Child Welfare Act of 1976 was a response to the large number of Native-American children who were being placed in non–Native-American foster homes or institutions. It gave tribal organizations much greater control over what happened to these children, with the intention of placing children in Native-American homes, either foster or adoptive. But the result has been much confusion and serious disputes between biological parents and tribal organizations. It also means that the adoption of Native-American children by other than Native Americans is a very chancy endeavor. There have been various congressional initiatives to clarify the situation, but they have all drowned in controversy. Relations between tribal organizations and the federal government are very troubled these days, and solutions seem hard to come by.

Maternity Leave for Adoptive Mothers

Q. I know several women who were given unpaid maternity leave when they had their babies, with a guarantee that a job would be held for them to return to. *Is maternity leave also available for adoptive mothers?*

A. Most companies that grant maternity leave would not make any distinction between a woman who was giving birth to a child and a woman who was adopting one, recognizing that the vital factor in both cases is the mother being in the home during the infant's formative months.

Health Insurance

Q. It looks as though we are finally going to get a child to adopt very soon. *Is an adopted baby covered by the health insurance of the adoptive parents or does he or she require a separate policy?*

A. In most states adopted children are treated the same as biological children if the adoptive parents have a family plan. If you do not have a family plan, you should switch to one immediately so that your baby will be covered from the moment of placement.

Adoption Rituals?

Q. I know something about open adoption, but I saw a piece on the subject on the television show *48 Hours* that made my jaw drop. A young couple was shown handing over their newborn baby to the adoptive parents surrounded by family and friends of both parties. It looked like a pagan ritual, complete with burning candles. *Are strange ceremonies normal in open adoptions?*

A. Ceremonies are not especially common, but it hardly seems fair to describe that particular event as a pagan ritual. To this viewer, it simply seemed that the biological and adoptive parents had gotten together to create a grand and loving occasion. The burning of candles outside of an established church does not turn the ceremony into something strange. It seems likely that the adoptive parents in this case were selected by the biological parents exactly because they were open to making this rite of passage into a special moment for all involved, including family and friends.

□:□:□:□:□ **90** □:□:□:□:□

Naming an Open
Adoption Baby

Q. We had the extreme good fortune to find and be chosen by the perfect birth mother. She is bright, pretty, and excited that we will become the parents of her baby. Over the past three months, we have practically become a family. But there is one problem. She has chosen a name for the baby. My husband and I have some very different names in mind. *Does our "almost perfect" birth mother have any legal rights when it comes to naming the baby?*

A. None. After the adoption papers have been signed, the baby can be named whatever you choose. Experts would advise you not to let this matter slide, however. You need to confront this issue now or it could become a festering problem further down the line. Have a "family" talk with her. Perhaps a compromise could be worked out in which the baby was given the birth mother's choice as a middle name. Or you could even use three names before the surname—as in George Herbert Walker Bush.

An Old Family Name

Q. We are adopting a baby boy and want to name him after my husband's maternal grandfather. He has four aunts on that side of the family and three of them are outraged at the very idea. They're saying, in essence, "How dare you name an *adopted* baby after my father!" *Is it improper to give an adopted baby a respected family name?*

A. Quite the contrary. An adopted child who is given the name of a great-grandparent is going to derive an extra measure of security from that fact; it reinforces the idea that he or she is part of a larger family. Your husband's aunts are way out of line here and clearly need some educating on the subject of adoption. Fortunately, attitudes like theirs often melt away once there is an actual baby around to coo over.

A Special Godmother

Q. After waiting for eighteen months, my husband and I are now the parents of a beautiful adopted baby girl. I can't begin to express how happy we are. However my aunt (my mother's only sister) has made life miserable for us because we did not ask her to be the baby's godmother. I don't think she would have objected as much if it had been an old friend of mine who was chosen. But we instead asked our caseworker, who has been enormously helpful and supportive from start to finish, to serve as godmother. She was thrilled to be asked. *Is it very unusual for adoptive parents to ask a caseworker to be the baby's godmother?*

A. Quite the contrary, it is surprisingly common. After all, a very supportive caseworker does more than anyone else to help the adoptive parents through the long process, keeping their spirits up and looking out for their interests. There are many instances of a caseworker and the adoptive parents becoming lifelong friends.

An Early Baby Shower?

Q. My son and his wife have been waiting seven months for an adopted baby. The waiting has been tension-filled for all of us. I thought I would lighten things up by having a baby shower for my daughter-in-law. *Would it be out of line to give a shower for an adopted baby in advance?*

A. Obviously you mean well, but to give a baby shower at this point would not only be in poor taste but also unintentionally cruel. The adoption process can take two to three times as long as seven months. For your son and daughter-in-law to have boxes of baby clothes and toys, and a huge supply of Pampers stacked in a closet, would only be a constant reminder of how long the wait is continuing. Save the baby shower until after they have gotten the child.

When's My Little Sister Coming?

Q. After a year on a waiting list to adopt a baby girl, we are getting very impatient and talk about the situation all the time. Our four-year-old adopted son seems to be having a hard time understanding the delay and keeps asking about when his sister will be arriving. *Is it a mistake to tell an older child of adoption plans in advance?*

A. An older child must of course be prepared for what is going to happen, but it shouldn't be done too far in advance. Remember that the adoption process can be very drawn out. For a four-year-old like your son, a month can seem like an eon. Parents should avoid creating anticipatory anxiety in an older child no matter how much they may feel it themselves.

When matters have progressed far enough so that it is clear there will be a new child in the family soon, begin preparing the older child for the grand event.

A Family Event

Q. My mother-in-law was horrified when I told her that we plan to take our five-year-old adopted son with us when we pick up his adopted baby sister. She went on and on about how it would be an emotional shock to her beloved only grandson. Right now, *I'm confused. Are we all wrong to make this joyful day a family affair?*

A. Absolutely not. You are doing the healthiest thing in the world for your son. This will give him a better understanding of the "mystery" of adoption. And making him feel a part of the event will help to smooth the transition to a new family dynamic. People who had a similar experience remember it as a very special day.

One detail to consider is where everyone sits in the car on the drive home. It's best if the older child gets to sit up front with the parent who is driving, while the other parent and the baby sit in back. That way the older child will not feel left out or get the sense that the baby is more important than he is.

The Adoption Secret

Q. Our adopted son is now three years old and has not been told he is adopted. We would like to keep it that way. We moved to another state right after the adoption took place, so no one where we live knows anything about the situation. My sister, however, tells us we are asking for trouble. *Have we made a mistake in not telling our son he was adopted?*

A. Almost all experts believe it is a major mistake not to tell a child he or she is adopted. Such secrets rarely remain undisclosed. The people in the town you live in now may not know, but your relatives and people you knew previously do. At some point, the truth is almost bound to come out, whether by accident or malicious design.

The emotional trauma of discovering later in life that you are adopted can take an enormous toll. Actor Jack Nicholson was stunned to discover in midlife that the woman he thought was his mother was really his grandmother and that his supposed sister was in fact his mother. He was mature enough to work through the shock, but if the discovery is made during the teenage years, the results can be tragic. There have been cases in which the child committed suicide, ran away, or suddenly took up drugs. And there are many more in which the parents who wanted to keep the truth buried have earned the lifelong animosity of their adopted child. You must start educating your son about his adoption immediately. Don't delay any longer.

Telling the Child

Q. The dreaded moment is at hand. I am speaking of telling our two-year-old that she was adopted. My husband and I have even rehearsed what we might say, but everything sounds stupid or way over her head. Obviously, we need help. *What do experts say is the most intelligent way to tell a child that he or she is adopted?*

A. This is probably the most asked question about post-adoption issues. Interestingly, large numbers of adopted people cannot remember being told they were adopted. They will shrug and say, "I can't remember not knowing. There was no big moment of discovery." This should give you a clue as to what needs to be done. It is not a matter of sitting the child down and making a "prepared statement." Rather, it is something that should be dropped into a simple chat with your child when it seems appropriate. Many adoptive parents start telling a child that he or she is adopted before the child has even reached the age to construct sentences. Experts do recommend that the word "adoption" be linked with the idea of being "chosen," and thus extra-special. But if the process of getting this idea across is carried out over time without making a big deal about it, the child will look back and say, "I've always known."

One Child Adopted, The Other Biological

Q. The birth of our now seven-year-old son was very difficult and I was strongly warned not to try to have more children. But we did want another child and felt it would be good for our son to have a younger brother. He seemed very pleased with the idea, but since the arrival of our adopted three-year-old son, our biological son has been behaving very badly toward his new brother. He even says things like, "You're not my real brother." *How unusual is our older son's reaction to his adopted younger brother?*

A. What seems terrific in the abstract to a child may not be nearly as welcome once it actually occurs. It is not unusual for an older biological child to resent the arrival of a younger sibling at first. But it is disturbing that he is attacking his new brother on the grounds of being adopted. You must put a stop to this. Most experts would suggest that you need to impress upon your older boy that his new brother needs him and his protection. Try to get this across not in terms of duty, but rather in terms of the older boy being a "grown-up" who can help his younger brother learn how to deal with the world.

"Quality Time"

Q. Although my husband was all for adopting a child, he is not paying very much attention to our five-month-old adopted daughter. This upsets me more than I can say. If I hear him say, "I give her *quality time*" once again I will scream. That remark makes me feel like my "quantity" time counts for nothing. I am giving our daughter both quality and quantity time about eighteen hours a day. *Is it the norm for a man to have so little interest in his adopted baby?*

A. No. Your husband must be a good actor, since adoption agencies are usually good at spotting this potential problem. The "quality time" concept has never held water. It is a dodge used by lazy or immature fathers (and sometimes mothers) whether the child is adopted or biological. Your husband needs to spend some "quality time" at the nearest post-adoption help meeting. These organizations can be found all across the country and can be of immense help in situations such as yours.

Post-adoption Counseling

Q. My older sister and her husband adopted a six-year-old boy. He's a cute kid in some ways, but he is also seriously hyperactive and they obviously are having trouble dealing with the situation. He was adopted through a state agency. *Do state agencies provide any kind of post-adoptive counseling, or does a couple have to seek out private help?*

A. A growing number of state agencies do provide post-adoptive counseling, especially for adoptions involving older children. More informal groups formed by adoptive parents can be very helpful with minor adjustments and with situations that arise with very young children. But the kind of problem your sister and her husband are experiencing is one better addressed by professionals.

Photos to India

Q. Good friends of ours adopted a baby from India about a year ago. Everything was completely legal, and the parents made two trips to India at their own expense in the course of the adoption process. No baby could ask for more loving care. Yet these adoptive parents are required to send photographs of the baby to the agency in India on a regular basis. *Why would a foreign adoption agency require photographic evidence of the baby's development?*

A. Some countries are suspicious of why Americans are so desperate to adopt their children. Even though the child would have had a much harsher life in his or her own country, agencies sometimes want to reassure themselves that the baby is being treated right, and not being abused in some way. Believe it or not, some of them are concerned about "child slavery." Photographs help to ease their fears.

Gifts from the Birth Mother

Q. Our five-year-old adopted son has always received birthday and Christmas gifts from his birth mother, forwarded through the adoption agency. This was fine with me at the beginning, but she has apparently married a fairly wealthy man, and the gifts have been escalating in value. For instance, for his recent birthday, she sent him a fifty-dollar bill. The situation is getting out of hand since we cannot afford to spoil *our* son in this way. *Is there any way to stop this woman from trying to one-up us with her gifts?*

A. Any responsible adoption agency should screen any correspondence between a birth mother and the child, and be willing to step in and insist that the value of any gifts be scaled back if you so request.

Grounds for Reclaiming a Biological Child?

Q. Two years ago I gave up my baby boy for adoption. The father had disappeared and I had no money and so no real choice. But I have recently married a man who is quite well-off and I would like to get my son back. My new husband is supportive of the idea. *Does the fact that I am now in a position to properly care for my child give me any grounds to try to get him back?*

A. No. If that sort of reason for reclaiming a baby given up for adoption prevailed, the entire system would be thrown into chaos. The most common legal grounds on which birth mothers try to regain a child is that of coercion—that the mother was coerced into agreeing to the adoption when she was not sufficiently strong emotionally or mentally to resist. But these cases can be extremely difficult to prove, and their validity lessens greatly over time. If a birth mother were to bring a suit claiming coercion within a very few months after the adoption was finalized, she might have a chance. But after a period of two years, such as in your own case, the courts are extremely reluctant to disrupt the by now settled relationship with the adoptive parents.

Feeling Like a Father
Much Too Late

Q. Six years ago I had a relationship with a girl for three years that began when we were seventeen. When she became pregnant, like a jerk I skipped town. I heard that she had twin sons, but I have never seen them. Now she is married and her husband is planning to adopt my boys. This is driving me crazy. They are my sons, after all, even though they were given their mother's last name. *Can I legally put a stop to the adoption of my sons by my former girlfriend's husband?*

A. Although you are the biological father, the chances of blocking the adoption are virtually nonexistent since you never established a relationship with the children. It is hard to imagine a judge who would not agree with your own statement that you behaved like a jerk, and you aren't likely to get any sympathy at this late date.

Wrongful Adoption

Q. My daughter and son-in-law adopted what they thought was a healthy baby boy two years ago. As it turns out, the boy is a victim of fetal alcohol syndrome and has physical problems as well as being retarded. My daughter and son-in-law love the child, but the expenses of raising him are obviously going to be much greater than expected. *Can they sue the agency for money damages because they were not told that the baby was brain-damaged?*

A. Yes, but only if the agency knowingly withheld medical information in its possession at the time of the adoption. These cases, which come under the heading of "wrongful adoption," are unusual, but do seem to be on the increase. There is often a debate about whether an agency did know there was a problem or simply should have known, on the basis of other information in its files—in cases of fetal alcohol syndrome, for example, the fact that the mother was drinking heavily throughout the pregnancy. Out-of-court settlements are quite often made in these cases.

Damaged Goods?

Q. A "perfect young couple" we know adopted what was thought to be a healthy baby. After placement, it was discovered that the baby was severely hearing-impaired, so they returned the child to the agency. This sounds to me like a case of a refund for damaged goods. This case makes me furious because one of my three children was born retarded, and it never once entered my mind to institutionalize him. *Is this kind of "return policy" usual in the adoption world?*

A. If an adopted child has a medical problem that the agency either knew about or should have been aware of, it is possible to return the child. Fortunately, there are quite a lot of adoptive parents who are a good deal more "perfect" than your young couple, who decide to keep a handicapped child even so. Such people have the maturity to recognize that if they had had a biological child, a similar problem could have existed, and see it as their responsibility to be loving parents to the child who has entered their lives regardless of any difficulties. It should be added that these adoptive parents would be regarded as prime candidates to adopt another child in the future.

Separated Siblings

Q. My wife and I did tons of research while waiting to adopt our daughter: counseling, weekly meetings with adoptive parents, and endless phone calls and letters to any organization that would respond to us. Two years after adopting our daughter at the age of three, we learned that she had a brother two years younger. We were informed of this fact by an anonymous source who we assume to be a caseworker trying to blow the whistle on her agency. Had we known about the little brother, we would gladly have adopted him too. *Isn't it a rule that siblings should not be separated?*

A. There are no absolute rules on the separation of siblings, but agencies do try very hard, in most cases, to see to it that they stay together. Unfortunately, few adoptive parents want to take on two children simultaneously. In your case, however, it sounds as though the agency seriously bungled the situation. You should certainly have been informed of the existence of the younger brother and given the opportunity to apply to adopt both children.

A Family Tree?

Q. I am so angry I can hardly see straight. My daughter's fifth-grade teacher asked her class to prepare a family tree over a weekend as a homework assignment. But she took my daughter aside after class and told her that she didn't have to do it since she was adopted. My daughter protested, saying that she knew a lot about her family tree and that we had portraits of her great-grandparents at home. The teacher said, "Well, if you want to, dear, but it's not the same thing." My daughter came home in tears. *Do the teachers' colleges in this country teach nothing about how to deal with a sensitive issue like adoption?*

A. There are many experts on education who feel that teachers' colleges, and all the red tape they involve, are the bane of American education. Some are much better than others, of course, and there are those that deal with the subject of adoption along with problems that can arise from racial insensitivity. But a lot of them are much more interested in Mickey-Mouse teaching techniques than they are in how to deal with real children. And it sounds as though your daughter's teacher is either a very stupid or a very prejudiced person.

Unfortunately, this kind of thing happens all the time, and adoptive parents have to be prepared. The very fact that your daughter had the gumption to protest suggests that you have done a very good job in making her feel that she is very much a part of an ongoing family history.

An Unnatural Mother?

Q. I am the proud mother of an adopted boy, Stephen, who is now five. The other day Stephen and I were at the mall window shopping while waiting to meet my husband for lunch. A neighbor came along with her visiting mother, who remarked how much Stephen looked like me. My neighbor immediately said, "Susan is not his natural mother." I've passed off such comments many times, but this time I let loose. "Does that make me his unnatural mother?" I snapped. "I'm quite sure I don't come from outer space." My neighbor hasn't spoken to me since. *Am I being oversensitive in so disliking the term "natural mother"?*

A. The tactless remarks people are capable of in respect to adoption are legion, and it is hardly surprising that adoptive parents sometimes lose patience. The term "natural mother" is severely frowned upon by adoption experts for reasons your sarcasm made very clear. But the best way to handle this is to try to educate people, telling them that the correct term to use is "biological mother." That still doesn't excuse your neighbor for making the remark at all, especially in the presence of your son.

Telling Off the Neighborhood Bully

Q. My six-year-old son is constantly being teased about being adopted by a little rat named Max, who is a classic neighborhood bully. My son takes it fairly well, all things considered, but I keep feeling there ought to be some way to put Max in his place. *Is there any good retort my son could make to stop this bully from teasing him about being adopted?*

A. Yes, there is. A number of adult adoptees have talked with considerable glee about the advice given them by their parents on how to handle this situation. It is not a "politically correct" solution, but sometimes it is necessary to fight fire with fire. Have your son say, "Yeah, well my parents chose me. Yours had to take what they got." This could lead to a fistfight, of course, but most adoptees say the bully was so stunned, he just slunk away.

A Talk with the Taunter's Parents

Q. Our five-year-old adopted daughter came screaming into the house in tears after being taunted by one of her little playmates. "She told me that I was ugly and that's why my real parents gave me away. Mommy, am I ugly?" My daughter is not Elizabeth Taylor in *National Velvet*, but she is far from ugly, and in fact a good deal prettier than the little girl who taunted her. I comforted and reassured my daughter as best I could, but I am still very angry. *In situations where an adopted child is being taunted, does it do any good to talk to the parents of the child who's being so mean?*

A. Sometimes, as in the case of the little boy who was teased by the neighborhood bully, it is enough to give your adopted child some return ammunition and let the child take care of it himself or herself. But there are situations in which it is necessary to confront the other parents. While most people don't like to admit it, children can be absolute little monsters on their own hook. But there are other situations where there's more to it. Biological parents can be smug and uninformed about adoption, and their attitude can rub off on their own "little darlings." If you are on at least relatively cordial grounds with the parents of your child's playmate, it can be worthwhile to call up and tell them what's going on. Try not to be accusatory, but rather to educate them a little on the subject of adoption. If they get their backs up, say you just thought they should know what had happened and don't press further, or you could have a minor war on your hands that your daughter would be caught in the middle of. As a bottom line here, ask yourself if you would call if the matter didn't involve adoption issues. That can give you some perspective.

Passport Problems

Q. Our fifteen-year-old adopted son has applied to a foreign exchange program, which means he will need a U.S. passport. The birth certificate provided by the agency has him listed under a "fictitious" name. *How should our son go about getting a birth certificate with his adopted name on it, or should we in fact do the applying for him?*

A. In terms of encouraging grown-up responsibility, it is an excellent idea to have him write a letter of application himself, but since he is not yet of legal age, it would be wise to include a cover letter of your own asking that your son's request be facilitated. He will need to give his date of birth and the name of the adoption agency involved. The letter should be addressed to the city hall in the town or city listed on the original birth certificate. Enclose a photocopy of the original certificate in your possession. A new certificate will be issued for a small fee, which you should call ahead to the bureau of records to determine.

Adopted Child Syndrome

Q. As a future adoptive grandmother, I have been reading everything I can find on the subject of adoption. In other words, I am doing my homework. But I came across a term in a magazine article that baffled me. *What is "adopted child syndrome"?*

A. This term refers to the wrongly negative light that adopted children are sometimes cast in. For instance, if an adoptee commits a crime, large or small, some people are likely to say, "What a pity about that child, Billy. But you know he's adopted. What can you expect?"

This kind of thinking, of course, is sheer prejudice, based on the myth that many children put up for adoption are in some way "defective." The fact is that adopted children are no more and no less likely to "get into trouble" than biological children.

An "Adopted" Doll

Q. My adopted daughter was given a Cabbage Patch doll by my husband's spinster oldest sister. Some people, the sister included, thought it was just adorable that the doll came complete with adoption papers. "What a perfect present for an adopted little girl!" was the cry. I was not at all amused. In my opinion, an "adopted" doll has no connection with the reality of adopting a flesh-and-blood baby. It trivializes the whole complex matter. *Am I being oversensitive in finding the whole idea of a doll with adoption papers disgraceful?*

A. Your outrage about Cabbage Patch dolls and their putative adoption papers has been shared by many adoptive parents and experts in the adoption field. All you can do is grit your teeth and recognize that we live in a society that tries to find a way to commercialize practically everything.

An Alcoholic Teenager

Q. Our sixteen-year-old adopted son is an alcoholic who is currently in a rehabilitative institution. I think I can truthfully say that we have been good parents, and we have never had alcohol in the house. But somehow he found ways to get hold of it. *Is it possible he inherited his alcoholism from his birth parents, and if so, can we sue the agency for not telling us that one or both of his parents were alcoholics?*

A. There is a good deal of evidence that alcoholism is hereditary, but it cannot be said that all children of alcoholics will develop the same problem. It is unlikely that you have grounds for a suit, however. Disclosure laws affecting adoption were far less strict in most states sixteen years ago than they are now, and if the boy's father had been an alcoholic but had disappeared before the mother even gave birth, as often happens, the agency might not have had the information anyway.

Bad Adoptive Parents

Q. I was adopted when I was a year old by a loving couple in Oklahoma. At least that was how everybody in town looked at it. But my loving mother never let me forget for an instant that I was "chosen" and therefore expected to be "perfect." "How dare you get a B in math? You were chosen." That kind of thing. My parents are very wealthy but I was never spoiled. My younger brother, also adopted, was treated very differently. The summer I was nineteen, I worked at JC Penney for extra money while my brother drove around town in a new red convertible my father had just given him for his seventeenth birthday. I am now twenty-six and hate my parents. *Am I being ungrateful in considering my parents to be far from the loving people everybody seems to think they are?*

A. Yours is a complicated story that needs to be looked at from two different angles. First, the way in which your mother berated you for not living up to the responsibility of being "chosen" is emotional child abuse. The concept of being chosen should be used only to bolster a child's confidence, never as a weapon to keep the child in line. Your mother's behavior is utterly reprehensible.

As to the different ways you and your brother were treated as you were growing up, it might be helpful to you to keep in mind that the kind of situation you describe occurs all the time in families with biological children. What it comes down to is that many people, no matter what their background, are not fit to be parents. And no one has to feel grateful for bad parents.

An Ungrateful Adoptee?

Q. Friends of ours adopted a nine-year-old girl. They had wanted an infant, but after waiting forever, they agreed to take an older child. The girl is very pretty, but she is a holy terror. She gives them endless problems and talks back to them in language that outdoes the most profane Hollywood movies. *How could an adopted older child be so ungrateful to her new parents?*

A. It seems very clear that this child comes from an abusive background. Such children can become so angry and bitter at an early age that they don't even *want* to be adopted. It takes a great deal of love and patience to break through to such a child, and some people do not have the strength for the job. But there are those who do, and there are a good number of cases that eventually have a happy ending. An abused child who can be made to understand that he or she is a cherished individual will in the long run offer a depth of gratitude that is almost beyond measure.

The Hidden Past

Q. I gave birth to a child as an unmarried teenager some twenty-five years ago and put the baby up for adoption. I was assured that the files would be sealed forever, and as a result I have never even told my husband of twenty years about the baby I bore so long ago. Now there seems to be a great deal of activity on the part of organizations helping adoptees to find their parents, and I have been worrying a lot lately that somehow the whole story will come out. *With changes in adoption laws and the push by several organizations to open all files, am I safe from the horror of having my past ripped open?*

A. You have little reason to worry. There is a push to open all files, but it is still being strongly resisted. About half the states have adopted a compromise, and new laws have established mutual consent registries to help biological parents and children find one another. But just as with the Adoptee's Liberty Movement Association (ALMA), these registries will not have you listed unless you request it. The state of Alaska has always had open files, and two other states, Kansas and Alabama, now have them, but they are not retroactive, so that files that were originally sealed remain so.

A Group Called ALMA

Q. I was adopted at birth by two wonderfully caring parents. I am now in my early thirties and they have both passed away in the past year. While they were alive, I didn't want to upset them by asking questions about my biological parents. But now that they're gone, I would like to investigate my biological roots. *How do I even start to find out something/anything about my biological mother and/or father?*

A. One method is to get in touch with the Adoptee's Liberty Movement Association (ALMA) (which means "soul" in Spanish). This organization has been reuniting adopted children with their biological mothers, fathers, and siblings with great success since 1971. ALMA maintains a computerized cross-indexed listing of adopted children and biological parents or siblings who are searching for one another.

Since membership in ALMA is voluntary, the organization can make a match only if both parties are registered. On a more controversial note, ALMA is also a leader in the fight to open the birth files of *all* adoptees.

Who Am I, Really?

Q. I am a fourteen-year-old adopted girl who wants to know who my real parents are. I love my adoptive parents a lot, but my real parents are part of me too. My adoptive parents don't see it that way. They say they are my "real" parents and there is no way to find out who gave birth to me, anyway. *How old do I have to be to legally find out who my birth parents are?*

A. You are at an age when children, adopted or not, are naturally trying to figure out who they are as people, and it is fairly common for an adopted child to feel that part of the answer lies in knowing who his or her biological parents were. But you are probably hurting your parents feelings by using the term "real parents." Look at it the other way around. How would you like it if your adoptive parents said you weren't their "real daughter"?

You will have to wait until you are eighteen (and in some states, twenty-one) before you can request that your name be put on a registry that might lead to finding your biological parents. But they won't be listed unless they want to find you too, which is not something you should count on. And by the time you are eighteen or older, you may not be interested anymore yourself—which is often the case.

The Uncurious Adoptee

Q. Both my older brother and I are adopted. He's thirty-five and I am twenty-nine. I want very much to find out who my biological parents are, but my brother couldn't care less about his. He's also quite cross with me because I brought the question up with my adoptive father (our adoptive mother died two years ago), who said he had no idea, all the files were closed. *Who's the strange one, me for wanting to know about my biological parents, or my brother for not caring?*

A. Neither of you is "strange," but the fact is that surprisingly few adopted children have any interest in their biological parents, with only about one in twenty making an active search. The public perception that large numbers of adopted children are searching for their biological parents is fueled by distorted news coverage. Newspapers and especially local television news programs are always on the lookout for human-interest stories and often make a big deal about reunions between adoptees and their biological parents or siblings. Such reunions are, however, decidedly uncommon events in terms of the overall adoption picture.

Child of Rape

Q. When I was a twenty-five-year-old married woman, I was raped in a parking lot. Being a devout Catholic, I never considered abortion. I carried the baby to term and put him up for adoption. My husband stood by me 100 percent throughout the whole horrible experience. I am now a fifty-eight-year-old grandmother. The emotional scars of the rape had pretty much disappeared until a couple of weeks ago. The son I had never wanted showed up on my doorstep. He was a nice-looking, well-spoken Hispanic young man. He said, "Nice to finally meet you, Mama." I tried to conceal my shock and invited him in. I asked him how he found me after all these years. He said that after a year of searching he had located the doctor who delivered him, who gave him my name, and then he spent another six months tracking me down. This may sound cruel, but I don't ever want to see him again. The wounds from my rape experience have been reopened, and I am a wreck. *Can I sue the doctor who gave out my name to the son I put up for adoption so long ago?*

A. You certainly can. The doctor's behavior is a very serious breach of medical ethics and, given your particular situation, simply unconscionable on any grounds. Fortunately, this kind of breach of professional conduct is rare, but your experience makes the case against having all adoption files open very clear.

Medical Information from Closed Files

Q. I am a married female who was adopted twenty-nine years ago. I am now expecting my first child. My problem is that my adoption files are sealed. It is very important for me to know my genetic background for the sake of my baby. *Is the need for medical information sufficient cause to get a birth file opened, and how do I go about it?*

A. You will have to file for a court order. All states have laws to give adoptees *needed* medical histories. But don't expect to receive any information that will give clues to your birth mother's identity, and be prepared to be turned down if you are just curious. There has to be a genuine need for information that a physician would require to deal with a particular problem.

Nonbiological Look-alikes

Q. My freshman roommate at college was adopted at birth. It was something he was very open about and obviously had no problems with. His parents lived across the country and I didn't meet them until recently at graduation. I was very surprised because Joe looks just like his father. It crossed my mind that he might in fact be his father's child by another woman. *How could a child unrelated by blood end up looking so much like one of his or her parents?*

A. Very easily. The operative phrase here is "end up." When an adopted child looks even a little like one parent or another—with eye color, high cheekbones, a prominent nose, whatever—the resemblance is likely to increase over the years as the child picks up various mannerisms from that parent and makes them his or her own. It is a subtle and complex process, but the result can be quite startling. It also happens, of course, among long-married couples who come more and more to look like one another. It has been pointed out that Jessica Tandy and Hume Cronyn, America's premiere husband-and-wife acting couple, could easily be mistaken for brother and sister at this point in their lives.

Adoptive parents and their children quite often run into comments about such resemblances from people who do not know that the child is adopted. Most of the time, the adoptive parents or adopted child just let the remark pass—exactly because of the kind of conclusion you leapt to about another woman!

Adopted Mother/ Biological Daughter

Q. I am a twenty-eight-year-old woman who was adopted at birth. I now have my own biological daughter, who has just turned three. I don't even remember not knowing I was adopted and am completely comfortable with it. But now I feel I need to explain to my daughter that I am adopted, and I feel curiously nervous about it. *Does it sometimes upset biological children to discover that their mother, or father, was adopted?*

A. There is no reason for them to be upset if they are told in a matter-of-fact way. There's no need to go into detail with a three-year-old, but it is likely your daughter will ask some questions of you when she gets older. One adopted woman tells of a wonderful conversation she had with her six-year-old biological daughter, who had asked to know more about what it meant to be adopted. The woman explained, and her daughter looked up at her and said, "I would have chosen you, too, Mommy."

A Note on Sources

The List of Adoption Organizations and the Bibliography that follow represent official sources consulted. But this book could not have been written without the enthusiastic participation of numerous individuals across the country. There were adopted children I have known from childhood or whom I encountered later in life who not only talked about their own experiences, but also put me in touch with other adopted individuals, as well as adoptive parents. Participants in local groups of adoptive parents in Florida's East Volusia County were extremely helpful, offering many insights into the problems and joys of the adoption process. To all these people, I am extremely grateful for their time and their openness.

List of Adoption Organizations

Adoptee-Birthparent Support Network
3421 M Street, N.W., Suite 328
Washington, D.C. 20007

Adoptees in Search, Inc. (AIS)
P.O. Box 41016
Bethesda, MD 20824

Adoption by Choice
4102 W. Linebaugh Avenue, Suite 200
St. Andrews Square
Tampa, FL 33624

The Adoption Center, Inc.
500 N. Maitland Avenue, Suite 305
Maitland, FL 32751

American Adoption Congress
1000 Connecticut Avenue, N.W., Suite 9
Washington, D.C. 20036

Americans for International Aid & Adoption
877 S. Adams Road
Birmingham, MI 48009-7026

Children's Defense Fund
122 C Street, N.W.
Washington, D.C. 20001

Concerned Persons for Adoption
P.O. Box 179
Whippany, NJ 07981

Holt International Children's Service
P.O. Box 2880
Eugene, OR 97402

National Adoption Exchange
1218 Chestnut Street
Philadelphia, PA 19107

National Adoption Information Clearinghouse
11426 Rockville Pike, Suite 410
Rockville, MD 20852

National Committee for Adoption (NCFA)
1930 Seventeenth Street, N.W.
Washington, D.C. 20009

National Foster Parent Association
226 Kitts Drive
Houston, TX 77024

Reunite, Inc.
P.O. Box 694
Reynoldsburg, OH 43068

Bibliography

Bunin, Catherine, and Sherry Bunin. *Is That Your Sister? A True Story of Adoption.* New York: Pantheon Books, 1976.

DuPrau, Jeanne. *Adoption.* Englewood Cliffs, NJ: Prentice Hall, 1981.

Edelman, Marion Wright. *Families in Peril: An Agenda for Social Change.* Cambridge: Harvard University Press, 1987.

————. *The Measure of Our Success: A Letter to My Children and Yours.* New York: Beacon Press, 1992.

Ford, Mary, and Joe Kroll. *Challenges to Child Welfare.* St. Paul, MN: North American Council on Adoptable Children, 1990.

Gilles, Tom, and Joe Kroll. *Barriers to Same Race Placement.* St. Paul, MN: North American Council on Adoptable Children, 1991.

Krementz, Jill. *How It Feels to Be Adopted.* New York: Knopf, 1982.

Leitch, David. *Family Secrets—A Writer's Search for His Parents and His Past.* New York: Delacort, 1984.

Lindsay, Jeanne Warren. *Open Adoption: A Caring Option.* Buena Park, CA: Morning Glory Press, 1987.

————, and Catherine Monserrat. *Adoption Awareness*. Buena Park, CA: Morning Glory Press, 1989.

McTaggart, Lynne. *The Baby Brokers*. New York: Dial Press, 1980.

Margolies, Marjorie, and Ruth Gruber. *They Came to Stay*. New York: Coward, McCann and Goeghegan, 1976.

National Committee for Adoption. *Adoption Factbook*. Washington, D.C.: National Committee for Adoption, 1989.

Powledge, Fred. *The New Adoption Maze*. St. Louis, MO: The C. V. Mosby Company, 1985.

Register, Cheri. *"Are Those Kids Yours?": American Families with Children Adopted from Other Countries*. New York: Free Press, 1990.

Rosenberg, Maxine B. *Growing Up Adopted*. New York: Bradbury Press, 1989.

Index